The Challenge of Living

Maximum Living Bereavement Guide

BY JOHN D. CANINE

BALL PUBLISHERS
Birmingham, Michigan

The Challenge of Living

ISBN 0-9755091-0-1

In Dedication to my Father and Mother,
David and Margaret Canine,
who challenged me in many areas of life.
I could have no better parents.

Acknowledgments

The greatest reward to a counseling professional and educator is to see learning, growth, change, and progress in the lives of the people I work with. These people enrich my life as I hope I do theirs.

For the focus, direction, and sometimes great debates which have shaped my beliefs and attitude toward grief and bereavement, I express my gratitude to the members of my doctoral committee: Dr. Arthur Brown, Dr. Leonard Kaplan, Dr. Harry Magoulias, as well as Dr. Nathaniel Champlin, Dr. Robert Craig, and Dr. Fred Neff.

Susan M. Anderson, M.Ed., provided assistance in writing and editing this guide book for which I am very grateful.

A big thank you goes to the typist, Jan Blain, who has worked very patiently with me through some very difficult times during the writing of my doctoral dissertation and this bereavement guide.

TABLE OF CONTENTS

Introduction 4

CHAPTER ONE: A LOOK AT DEATH — THE BACKGROUND 5
Recognizing Stress 7
Distorting Our View of Death 9
Denying and Accepting Death —
The Push and the Pull 10
Prolonging Life and Working Against Nature 12
Viewing Immortality 14

CHAPTER TWO: DEATH AWARENESS 17
Improving Your Quality of Life 18
Coping Effectively With Emotions About Death ... 21
Defining Social Issues that Personally Affect You 22
Encouraging Anxiety 24

CHAPTER THREE: STEPS FOR SURVIVAL 27
Acknowledge Death 29
Understand and Accept the Pain 31
Realize Your Suffering Is Not Unique 32
Work Through Your Guilt 33
Feel Good About Yourself — You Are a Survivor .. 37

CHAPTER FOUR: HABITS FOR GOOD HEALTH 41
Be Kind to Yourself 42
Be Positive 44
Relieve Your Anger 45
Take Care of Your Body 47
Record Your Thoughts as You Recover 50

CHAPTER FIVE: GOALS FOR GROWTH 51
Make Changes 52
Be Forgiving 54
Help Others 56
Let the Past Brighten Your Future 57
Discover Your Creative Self 59

Introduction

Learning about death can improve the quality of your life. In essence, the goal of this bereavement guide is to enrich your life. All of us will anguish over death at some point in our lives and need to put this learning to work.

We suffer from ignorance, fear and misconceptions about death. Most of us have not considered how our own deaths would affect the lives of those we love: we have difficulty contemplating our own mortality.

In this guide we will explore death from our denial of death through the grief process and on to the transformation and shifting of our own values as we look at death to improve our own lives. Hopefully, this guide contains ideas to assist learning and growth for all readers.

CHAPTER ONE

A LOOK AT DEATH — THE BACKGROUND

*I want them to show me where the
way out Exists for this captain
shackled by death.*
— Federico Garcia Lorca

- Recognizing Stress
- Distorting Our View of Death
- Denying and Accepting Death —
  The Push and the Pull
- Prolonging Life and Working
  Against Nature
- Viewing Immortality

Stress Through Loss

Stress Through Work

RECOGNIZING STRESS

If you have suffered the loss of someone close to you, how you might feel and why you might feel that way are important things to think about. You need to be concerned about yourself. Your life is changed. The challenge is to gradually accept this change and move your own life forward.

First, you must recognize that death is a stress-producing event. "Stress" can be defined as a mentally or emotionally upsetting state. If you look at the following list of stressful events, you will see that death holds a high position, and that eight of the first ten events are related to a person's loss. Take a minute to add up the numbers on the scale that are next to events that have happened to you in the last year.

Life Change Index

Event	Scale of Impact
Death of Spouse	100
Divorce	73
Marital Separation	65
Jail Term	63
Death of Close Family Member	63
Personal Injury or Illness	53
Marriage	50
Fired From Job	47
Marital Reconciliation	45
Retirement	45
Change in Health of Family Member	44
Pregnancy	40
Sex Difficulties	39
Gain of New Family Member	39
Business Readjustment	39
Change in Financial State	38
Death of Close Friend	37
Change to Different Line of Work	36
Spouse (arguments)	35
Mortgage over $40,000	31

Foreclosure of Mortgage or Loan 30
Change of Responsibilities at Work 29
Son or Daughter Leaving Home 29
Trouble with In-Laws 29
Outstanding Personal Achievement 28
Spouse Begins or Stops Work 26
Begin or End School 26
Change in Living Conditions 25
Revision of Personal Habits 24
Trouble with Boss 23
Change in Work Hours or Conditions 20
Change in Residence 20
Change in Schools 20
Change in Recreation 19
Change in Church Activities 19
Change in Social Activities 18
Mortgage or Loan Less than $40,000 17
Change in Sleeping Habits 16
Change in Number of Family Get-Togethers .. 15
Change in Eating Habits 15
Vacation 13
Christmas 12
Minor Violations of the Law 11
Total

If your total on the Scale of Impact is more than 300, you might be close to severe depression or even a mental or physical illness. By recognizing the degree that stress can affect you, you will be able to:

- Protect yourself from other kinds of stress.
- Make the stress work for you.

In his book, *Stress Without Distress,* Hans Selye says that "stress is the spice of life." If this is true, then people can use the steam produced by their stress to move their emotional engine, rather than blow it up. In this sense, stress can be either a positive or negative force. Since you cannot avoid it, and it can destroy you, the key is to identify your stress and channel your energy in a positive direction. You have suffered a loss: How can you make the stress from your loss work for you?

DISTORTING OUR VIEW OF DEATH

You may have to work hard to deal with your personal loss because our culture does not let us "look at" death. One hundred years ago when cities were small villages, most people had no choice but to be involved with someone's death. Family members and friends were always present when a person died and nearly everyone participated in the funeral rites.

Today, we are not so intimate. Reviewing the obituary column in the newspaper or receiving a phone call that a friend or relative died is about as close as we may come to death. Many people die alone whether they are at home, in the hospital, or on the road. Attendance at the funeral might be minimal, or there might not be any funeral at all — just a cremation. In fact, people may give their casual yet guarded attention to death through American's most popular medium — the television. Perhaps you remember the dramatic series, "Run for your Life." The scenario went something like this, a middle-class husband arrives home one evening to find his wife murdered. Enraged by this, he spent the rest of the series pursuing the alleged murder suspect: the one-armed man. This death-related theme is common to television detective stories and spy novels. Marc Golden, formerly in charge of program development at CBS, states:

> There's one constant in every successful dramatic TV story form and that's that the leading character's occupation is somehow connected with death . . . . I don't know why, but story forms connected with death are the only ones that home audiences are willing to watch in numbers large enough to make a dramatic series economically viable.

We would rather keep death at an "arm's length" partly because our society is prudish about death. Most people are squeamish about death, viewing it as a disgusting, immoral subject not to be discussed in polite company. We try to ignore death so we won't have to come to terms with either our own human responses or with death as part of our lives. The fact is we need to come to terms with death. If we choose to ignore this need, the end result is a fascination with bizarre death stories. If we avoid dealing with our normal feelings of sorrow, guilt and love at the occasion of death, the harsh, brutal deaths of fiction capture the feelings we cannot deal with.

DENYING AND ACCEPTING DEATH — THE PUSH AND THE PULL

You might find it curious to know that people in our culture both deny and accept death at the same time. You might be able to accept someone else's death, yet deny that some day you too will die. In fact, any loss by death does two things: it reaffirms the fact that you are alive; it reaffirms the fact that you will die.

Noted author-psychiatrist Kubler-Ross views a person's reaction to his or her own death as both Denial and Acceptance of death with three stages in-between: Anger, Bargaining and Depression. As you read the following, relate these stages to your own thoughts about death:

Denial — When you deny your own death (as when told you have a terminal illness), your reaction might be, "It cannot be true." This is a temporary response that allows you time to collect yourself and deal rationally with your situation.

Anger — You are angry because this is happening to *you*. You are envious and resentful of those who will live. You might say, "Why couldn't this happen to George? He doesn't deserve to live." You find yourself striking out at family members, doctors, and nurses. Anyone who comes near you may feel your anger.

Bargaining — You have accepted your situation and are now looking to "extend the lease." You want to postpone your death and you begin to bargain, most often with God, to give you time to live for your "good behavior." You might say, "If I can just live through Mary's graduation next Spring, then I won't ask for anything else."

Depression — You are depressed about your loss of personal life. The purpose of this emotional state is to prepare you to accept your death. The depression may spill over into other areas of your life: you may be depressed about the loss of a job, money, your future dreams, or friends. You are reacting to what is happening to you.

Acceptance — You may be void of almost all feeling at this time. It's not that you have "given up," but you need time to rest before the end. Your interests may diminish and you may desire to be left alone in silence. Your family may need more help, patience and understanding than you do.

As you can see, Kubler-Ross makes dying much more than just an event. She wraps denial and acceptance around other emotional phases which she sees as part of dying.

If you were terminally ill, it would certainly be enough just to deal with your own emotions about your approaching death. However, that daily struggle is more complicated by the fact that, like you, others are having trouble dealing with their own acceptance or denial of your pending death. In survey results reported by Michael Simpson in the book *Dying*, 80% of the general population and all physicians polled said they *would* want to know if they were terminally ill. On the other hand, 90% of the physicians polled said they

11

would rarely, if ever, tell patients they were terminally ill. You might conclude from the survey that if you wanted to know about your terminal illness, the physician might deny you that right.

PROLONGING LIFE
AND WORKING AGAINST NATURE

A century ago when dying was an event in which almost everyone participated, a person became ill, the illness worsened, and the person died. Usually a person was not ill long enough for the family to have to agonize through a "waiting period" for death.

Today, the process of dying can last a long time. It has created what might be called a "new face" of death. Why is this? First of all, a high level of medical knowledge provides an early detection of fatal conditions or diseases. In addition, we now know that some diseases will lead to an earlier than normal death. What this means is that a terminally ill patient might "know" for a long time — months or even years — that he/she is dying. Secondly, the rate of death due to accidental injury lowers every year. Thirdly, if a patient is chronically ill or severely harmed in an accident, then doctors, nurses, and hospital policy stand ready to keep that person alive. And finally, because hospitals place a high value on extending a person's life, the process of defining a patient as dead can be difficult. A person could be "brain dead" but still have a beating heart. Or his body could be alive only with the help of a machine. Therefore, who has the right to and what are the conditions that define death?

In summary, one could assume that later in this century very few people will die of accidental injury. We probably will die from a chronic or fatal illness but not before hospitals and technology do everything possible to try to keep us alive.

How does this affect your quality of life? It means that a larger portion of life will be lived during the general decline of your physical condition. A study of four hundred males revealed that between the ages of thirty and seventy-five (about 60% of one's life) a man's average physical loss is as follows:

Old age is part of the process of dying.

Item Changed	Percent Lost
Brain weight	44%
Blood flow to the brain	20%
Cardiac output	30%
Kidney plasma flow	50%
The number of nerve trunk fibers	37%
Nerve conduction velocity	10%
The number of taste buds	64%
The maximum oxygen uptake during exercise	60%
The maximum voluntary breathing capacity	57%
Strength of hard grip	45%
Basic metabolic rate	16%
Total body weight	12%

You have read that hospital policy will work to keep you alive while your body declines physically. You may want to give some thought to your own control and exercising your own control over the quality of your life.

VIEWING IMMORTALITY

Perhaps the most asked question of all time is, "Does a life exist beyond death?" It is difficult to separate immortality from religion and it is a fact, according to the Gallup Poll, that 67% of the American public believes in life after death. From this 67% we know the following:

100% use religious terminology to describe the next life.
26% believe there will be no more problems in the next life.
21% believe it will be a better life.
16% believe it will be a peaceful life.
15% believe there will be no pain in the next life.
15% believe the next life will be happy, joyful, and without any sorrow.

What cannot be denied is that there is great human hope for immortality. Those who have been near death and then live claim experiences of passage to another life where they see "bright lights of peace" or pass through "dark tunnels." These claims are so strong and numerous that wondering about their meaning is thought provoking.

Many of us are looking to the after life for peace, joy, happiness, and the absence of pain. Perhaps it is this looking beyond to immortality that allows us to look at death at all.

CHAPTER TWO

DEATH AWARENESS

*Often the test of courage is not to die
but to live.*

— *Alfieri*

- Improving Your Quality of Life
- Coping Effectively With Emotions
  About Death
- Defining Social Issues that
  Personally Affect You
- Encouraging Anxiety

IMPROVING YOUR QUALITY OF LIFE

Most people in today's world find it easy to openly discuss most moral and social issues with each other. Newspapers, magazines, and other assorted reading materials boldly print the details of almost any topic. Television provides an open forum for even the most intimate concerns. Despite this candid flow of communication, there remains one subject that still hides in the shadows: the subject of death.

Whether it be the death of a loved one or a personal death, most people find it an unpleasant, undesirable task to come face to face with death. It is the purpose of this book to broaden your knowledge and understanding of death — to develop your death awareness. As the facts unfold, death awareness will help you accept death with little or no fear. Removing fear of death will enable you to do four things: 1) improve your quality of life, 2) cope effectively with your emotions about death, 3) define social issues that personally affect you, and 4) encourage an anxiety to stimulate your thinking.

Accepting and understanding death is the first step toward improving the quality of your life. Once you have accepted the certainty of death, death can then perform a function: it can act as a stimulus for examining and rearranging your own values and priorities in an effort to enrich your life. In this sense, death is not an end in itself, rather it is the impetus or the beginning of a new and better kind of living. The implications of death are therefore interwoven with life to create a more meaningful existence. This concept is illustrated best in the way terminally ill patients change their attitudes toward their lives once they have accepted the fact that death is near. In her book *To Live Until We Say Goodbye*, Kubler-Ross wrote about Beth, a 42-year-old New York model who discovered a new meaning in life once she had accepted her impending death:

What Beth demonstrated to us is that when human beings have the courage to face their

Sometimes Death Awareness is an afterthought.

own finiteness and come to grips with that deepest agony, questioning, turmoil and pain — they emerge as new people. They begin to converse with God, or the Source, or whatever you want to call it, and a new kind of existence begins for them. We have seen this in countless cases. These patients often become poets; they become creative beyond any expectations, far beyond what their educational backgrounds had prepared them for.

This process is exemplified in Beth by some of the thoughts that demonstrate the kind of person she became.

The following are two excerpts from Beth's diary:

It is nice to go out and walk in the sunshine, it just feels good to be alive and aware.

I used to wish for death
A lot of the time
Then I died
For a little time
Now I wish to die
Some of the time.
But, now I know
It will be
For all the time.

This concept of using your acceptance of death to improve your quality of life is called authenticity. Basically, it means you are a genuine, real person because you see death for what it is and you live a more meaningful life as a result. In other words, if you refuse to accept death as something that will inevitably happen to everyone, death can have no positive effect on your life. This story will help you understand how death can positively influence your life:

Bill is a well-organized man who usually lays out a plan for whatever he wants to accomplish each week. One day Bill's sister died from a severe illness. Her death was not only painful for him, but also scared him. Suddenly he found himself thinking about how long it would be before he too would die. Would he become seriously ill? Would he die from an unexpected accident? Suppose he only had a short time to live. If this were true, should he rethink the rest of his short life? Bill began to think about what was really important to him. He realized he might have to make some changes to achieve the things he most wanted to do. If only he knew how long he would live . . . .

The death of Bill's sister caused him to rethink what was important in his own life. He decided to rearrange his priorities so his life would be more meaningful. In doing this, Bill became more realistic about what was important in his life. He made a sincere, genuine effort to discover life for what it really was. When he accomplished this, he greatly improved the quality of his life.

The whole point of death awareness is to make a person so aware of his own potential death that a "new" individual emerges, an individual who sees life from a more meaningful perspective. Because this person's sense of value has changed or deepened, his new view of life makes him "creative beyond any expectations," and he experiences a fuller existence.

COPING EFFECTIVELY WITH EMOTIONS ABOUT DEATH

Death acceptance is the key to coping effectively with your emotions about death. To fear death is to keep it locked in the closet. To accept death is to bring it into the open thus removing your fear. It is the purpose of death awareness to unlock the doors of communication allowing people to share with each other their thoughts and feelings about death. This interaction can help all people learn to cope with their grief and bereavement.

A wide range of emotions arise when a person is confronted with the death of others or a personal death. Even if one manages to accept death, one still might be frightened about his/her personal reaction to that death. Every person reacts to death in a different way, so don't be surprised if your emotions come out in some unexpected fashion. For example, one man tells an intimate story about his wife's surprising reaction to her mother's death:

I recall the night my mother-in-law died. It was a sudden death and a shock to our family. Before the funeral my wife and I barely talked about her mother's death. Then, the evening following the funeral, my wife desperately wanted to make love, which we did. From that night on, she openly discussed her feelings about her mother's death. Since then, a psychologist friend told us that making love is not only the highest form of self-expression, but a natural, healthy response to the death of a loved one.

No matter how you feel, it is important to accept any emotional expression as a healthy outlet for your grief. Cry, scream, run, jump rope, make love. Do whatever has to be done to relieve the pain of your sorrow.

Death awareness helps you deal with these emotions through learning and sharing in an unthreatening environment. This is where the healing process begins, then you are on your way to effectively coping with your personal loss.

DEFINING SOCIAL ISSUES
THAT PERSONALLY AFFECT YOU

The function of death awareness can be extended to clarifying and understanding social and ethical issues that affect you personally. These issues can be confronted only if you can remove your fear of death. Then you will be able to talk about death on an intellectual level rather than an emotional one. Every day there are choices to make involving such personal values as work, play, drugs, and sex that have

What is the value of war?

both immediate and long-range consequences. At the same time, there are broader social problems that affect your life like pollution, war, abortion, overpopulation, capital punishment, and so on. Because so many of these issues center around death, a fear of death will keep you from dealing with them. Death awareness can relieve your fear allowing you to talk openly with others about these issues in an attempt to clarify and solve them.

The following are examples of questions that you can discuss with others to determine a set of values that you can apply to both personal decisions and societal choices:

1. Am I doing things that might cause me or others to die unnecessarily and prematurely?
2. What responsibility do I have for overpopulation?
3. Who in our society shall be allowed to use life-prolonging devices?
4. Considering the scarcity of land, should we continue allotting burial plots for every person?
5. Is there something I should do to help get rid of environmental pollution?
6. What is the value of war?

ENCOURAGING ANXIETY

Another reason to learn more about death is to make you aware of the anxiety death creates within you about your life. What does that mean? First of all, you already know that death means your time on earth is limited. Everyone has a built-in anxiety about that fact. It's an anxiety that says you only have so much time to do whatever it is you want to do while you are still alive. Therefore, that anxiety will cause you to question your life and set priorities and values that will improve the quality of your life. Your tendency is to escape from this anxiety. Better you face this anxiety, use it to improve your life, and, as a result, enjoy the chance to live life to its fullest.

Anxiety becomes the tool that each person uses to carve the future. In order to use this anxiety, one must, through his inner strength, be able to stand alone and take charge of his own destiny. During our childhood, we all learn to depend on other people or things to support our existence, whether it be family, friends, drugs, etc. Although this support system permits us to believe in ourselves, it is temporary. For example, when a friend dies, you lose some of your emotional support. This means you were living partly on borrowed power — you borrowed the inner strength of your friend to help maintain your own existence. Rather than borrowing from people and things around you, the challenge is to symbolically sever these social power lines and depend on your own inner strength to create your own power. When you are forced to stand alone to cope with your own weaknesses, you are motivated to understand and use your own creative and generative power. When this happens, you are in full possession of yourself. You have successfully pulled together all the aspects of your existence to make you a strong, independent individual.

CHAPTER THREE

STEPS FOR SURVIVAL

If I die, it will be glory;
if I live, it will be grace.
— *Justice William O. Douglas*

- Acknowledge Death
- Understand and Accept the Pain
- Realize Your Suffering Is Not Unique
- Work Through Your Guilt
- Feel Good About Yourself —
  You Are a Survivor

Acknowledge death.

ACKNOWLEDGE DEATH

There are many things we do not know about death because of the mystery that surrounds death itself. However, it is possible to know and understand our personal feelings about death whether it be our own death or the death of a close friend or relative. Then, and only then, can we begin to cope with the sadness and great sense of loss that follows the death of a loved one.

So — we *can* deal with what we *do* know. And the first step is to realize what has actually happened. Instead of asking yourself questions that cannot be answered like "Why did he have to die?" or "Why has this happened to me?", come to grips with reality and accept the fact that the death *has* occurred. Then decide what you are going to do to cope with your loss. With this in mind, consider the following suggestions:

Accept the fact of death.

It may be hard to believe this person has been taken away from you, but it's important to face the fact that it *has* happened.

Don't be afraid of death.

As with most people, it is possible that you fear death because you fear the unknown. But more than that, the loss of a companion creates a deeper fear of what will happen to *you* as a result of this loss. Remember, the death of someone important in your life means that part of your emotional support system has been cut off. Your fear is that the void will not be filled. However, as you begin to understand your grief, your fears will subside and that empty feeling will disappear.

Allow yourself to feel the loss.

Accept the fact that your suffering is painful. Go ahead

Admit that you are hurting.

and feel sad or angry. It's O.K. to feel these emotions, and it's even better to openly express them. Allowing your body to emotionally and physically react to the pain you are feeling is one way of releasing the pain from your system.

Expect that you might be in shock.

Some people react to a personal loss with no feeling at all. This emotional numbness might frighten you, but it's really just another way the human system copes with tragedy, especially sudden tragedy.

UNDERSTAND AND ACCEPT THE PAIN

Once you have become fully aware that your friend or relative's death has occurred and you have realized the fact that you are indeed suffering a loss, the next move along the road to recovery is to understand and accept the pain you are suffering. Spend some time thinking about the pain. Then ask yourself exactly what it is about your loss that is causing the pain. This is one way of getting in touch with your feelings — an important step in understanding your pain. As you try to understand and accept your pain, keep these things in mind:

Admit you are hurting.

One of the best ways to do this is to actually tell someone that you are hurting and how much you are hurting. The sound of your own voice expressing your grief will make these feelings more real to you.

Realize that pain is normal.

The fact that you are feeling something, having an emotional reaction, is proof of the living energy of your own being. It is a sign of the vital and healthy qualities existing in your body that are so necessary to the healing process.

Do not fear your pain.

At first, the sense of pain might frighten you. But if you are willing to feel the pain, you will discover that it is not bottomless. Pain does not have to control you. You have the power to control pain. So, let the pain come over your body and get in touch with its sensation.

See pain as a step toward healing.

Remember, pain is the beginning of the healing process. To run from pain would destroy any chance for recovery. Be realistic and remind yourself the pain is only temporary.

Recognize your inner strength.

The human body is much stronger than we know. Therefore, your own basic strength will help you withstand the kind of suffering that comes with a personal loss.

Survive the pain.

Expect that you will have pain, that it will hurt, and that it will cause you to be sad or angry. But also know that, because of your built-in strength, pain is something you can tolerate. And, although it might be tough, you *will* be able to survive the period of suffering.

REALIZE YOUR SUFFERING IS NOT UNIQUE

If you are reacting as so many others do, you very likely feel alone in the tragedy of your personal loss. You are caught in a web of sorrow, feeling heavy with grief. As you go about your daily activities, you feel distant from the people around you, alone in your despair. Your loneliness comes not only from your great sense of loss, but also from the notion that no one else shares your unhappiness. If this is how you feel, these two thoughts might be of help:

32

Death, bereavement, and loss of a loved one is something everyone must face.

It is possible that you are the only one you know that has been stricken with this particular tragedy, but rest assured that every day people around the world are suffering a similar personal loss of their own. Although it might be hard to imagine, all those other people are feeling the same emptiness that has shaken you. In varying degrees, they all share the same questions you are asking: "What will I do now?", "Where will I go from here?", "How can I live on without my loved one?". In this sense, your suffering is not unique. Take comfort in the fact that many people have had the same empty feeling you are having. What is happening to you is common, so you need not think your painful feelings are strange or unnatural.

Your friends can be a great comfort to you.

Be willing to talk to your friends about your grief. Their comfort and support are important to your emotional health. Often, your friends are uncertain about what will comfort you. So accept whatever they say as an attempt to help you feel better.

WORK THROUGH YOUR GUILT

Guilt can have a powerful effect on one's ability to cope with a personal loss. Often times a situation occurs just before a death in which an argument or some other conflict takes place between two people. Then, before they can "clear the air," one person dies and the other is left feeling guilty about what he/she might or might not have said to the deceased person. When this happens, it is important to realize that, although it might not be possible to completely remove the guilt from your conscience, you don't have to let it interfere with your quality of life. Here are some examples to help you understand this point:

Guilt can arise from an unintentional action.

John's mother had suffered for years from a serious illness. Confined to a wheel chair, she was very depressed about her declining physical condition. One day she told John her life would be much brighter if she could have fresh flowers in her room every day. John vowed he would fulfill her request and, although he meant to do so, he kept forgetting to order the flowers. A week later John's mother took a turn for the worse and died suddenly. John was not only saddened by her death, but devastated by the fact that he had forgotten to order her flowers. John didn't mean to disregard his mother's request. He simply forgot — and then it was too late. Even though it was unintentional, he had strong guilt feelings about neglecting his mother's request.

Guilt can result from an intentional action.

One summer morning Mary was angry at her 10-year-old son for not cleaning his room the previous day. She scolded him for not being responsible and demanded that he clean his room when he returned from a shopping trip with his uncle. Unfortunately, Mary's son died in an auto accident on the way home when a truck ran into his uncle's car. Mary grieved that she had been so angry that morning and did not have the chance to make amends with her son. She had intended to create a conflict with her son only to help him learn responsibility. Now she carried with her the guilt of those last angry words.

Again, it might not be possible to completely remove the guilt, but it is possible to understand your guilt and work through the problem.

Forgiveness can help remove guilt.

If you and a deceased friend had bitterness between you, try to think about that friend forgiving you — and you forgiving that friend. This must be done because the outcome of an unforgiving attitude is more guilt and pain.

Remember that God forgives.

If He forgives, you can too. In Christianity, God forgave Man through Jesus Christ. For Christians, following His example will bring you peace of mind.

Others forgive us.

Others forgive us when we least expect it.

Perhaps it's easy to forgive someone who has died, but you find it hard to forgive someone who is living because you think he/she will not forgive you. You might be surprised to find that if you express your forgiveness to someone, that person will be relieved to express his/her forgiveness to you.

The future can "even things out."

Perhaps you felt wronged by a deceased person before he/she died. Then later, after death, you learned that this person previously had done some special thing for you. Perhaps this person had talked to others about your terrific personality, or had been influential in your recent job promotion, or had recommended you for a scholarship . . . The future, if given the chance, can disclose many wonderful qualities about a person that would make up for any prior ill will. The future *can* even it all out.

Time heals all wounds.

As we move toward the future, away from the past, forgiveness becomes easier. Time can help you put your feelings in proper perspective.

Guilt can turn bad into good.

A confusing statement? Here's how it works. Guilt produces pain. When we feel pain, we ask questions and try to understand that pain. The questions inspire us to take action to heal the pain. Then by taking the proper action, the pain is overcome. If you can complete that process, you will have achieved three important goals. You will have:

1) accomplished a difficult task,
2) nursed yourself back to health,
3) greatly improved your quality of life.

FEEL GOOD ABOUT YOURSELF —
YOU ARE A SURVIVOR!

The stress that is created by the anger and sadness of a personal loss causes fatigue and lowers your resistance to almost everything. Like a battery that has run out of energy, your system has to be recharged. Feeling good about yourself can provide just the physical and mental boost you need. The following thoughts can lift your spirits:

Tell yourself you are O.K.

Your self-esteem may have suffered a jolt from the loss of your relative or friend. It's important to be kind to yourself reminding yourself of your good qualities. Talk to others about yourself in a positive way.

Avoid dwelling on your bad traits.

Thinking about your negative qualities can only result in wasted time and energy. You need to direct that time and energy into feeling good about yourself. Dwelling on your bad points will depress you.

Thoughts of guilt, worry, and self-doubt are only SYMPTOMS OF STRESS.

These anxious thoughts will add to your pain, so see them for what they really are: common symptoms of stress.

Avoid any thought that begins with "If only . . ."

Be aware of what you are thinking. Alert yourself to thoughts that begin with "If only . . .". For example, "If only I had seen her before she died . . ." or "If only I had told him how much I cared about him . . .". These thoughts will do just one thing: heighten your sense of guilt.

Pain can harm your self-image.

The pain you are suffering can cause you to see yourself in a poor light. Remember, the stress from pain causes fatigue that opens you to depression. Take time to remind yourself of all your good qualities.

The Road to Recovery is up and down.

You WILL get better.

Realize that you have what it takes to survive this unhappy time. Direct your thoughts toward a speedy recovery remembering that the healing process has a beginning, a middle and an end.

Healing takes time.

Expect the healing of your wounds will take some time. The pain will not go away immediately. But it *will* diminish as the weeks go by. Also keep in mind that the greater the loss, the more time it will take to heal your pain.

Take the time to heal your pain.

With automation and computers, our lives have become more convenient and we are able to do more in a shorter period of time. Generally, Americans live on a fast track expecting most things to happen quickly or even immediately. Be careful that these attitudes do not interfere with your healing process. It takes *time* to heal, so allow your system to heal at its own rate.

The healing process involves progress and setbacks.

As you advance along the road to good health, there probably will be events that will interrupt your progress. Don't let these setbacks discourage you. They are necessary to the healing process. This figure illustrates what you want to happen versus what does happen.

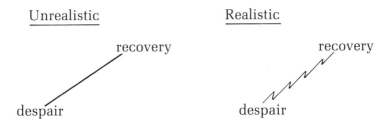

If you keep your mind focused on your recovery, the rough road will become smooth.

CHAPTER FOUR

HABITS FOR GOOD HEALTH

*No man enjoys the true
taste of life but he who
is willing and ready to
quit it.*
— Seneca

- Be Kind to Yourself
- Be Positive
- Relieve Your Anger
- Take Care of Your Body
- Record Your Thoughts as You Recover

BE KIND TO YOURSELF

Building one's self-esteem holds a primary position throughout the healing process. Because the stress of your sorrow and grief can cause depression, your ego needs constant refueling. You need a pat on the back, an arm around your shoulder in comfort. Imagine how good that would feel. The warmth you feel from gentle care does more for your sense of well-being than anything else in the world. This tender stroking can come from within you as well as from others. It's important to realize just how much you can care for yourself. A good way to start is to take time to think over your good features right down to the fine details. List those worthwhile qualities on paper. Then, on days when you're feeling especially blue, you can read over the list to give yourself a boost. Other hints to follow are:

Be gentle to yourself.

Give yourself time to mourn. Accept the emotions that are overwhelming you and express them. Try to get plenty of rest and exercise. Remember, the stress from a personal loss causes fatigue. You need rest and/or sleep to keep up your strength. Pamper yourself in small ways to brighten your spirits.

Treat yourself as you would a good friend.

Give yourself the same special care you would offer a good friend. Keep yourself well groomed, be patient, be considerate, be accepting, be forgiving.

Live one day at a time.

Don't be in a rush to recover immediately from your sorrow. Take life one day at a time, pacing yourself slowly and calmly so the healing process can run its full course. Live for the present not for next month or next year.

Avoid accepting "new" jobs or chores.

Let your boss know you are in a period of bereavement, that your sadness is causing unusual fatigue, and that it

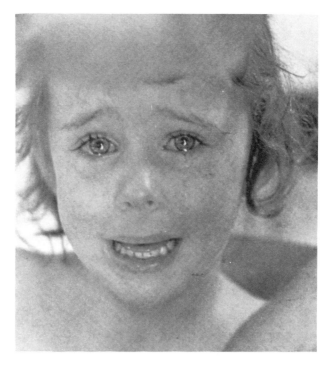

Cry long enough

. . . then move along.

would be hard for you to take on extra responsibilities. Hold off on any chores at home that can wait. Be careful not to overload or over-extend yourself.

Avoid stressful situations.

You already have a certain amount of stress from your loss. Beware of getting involved in situations that might cause you to overreact, thereby putting even more stress on your system.

BE POSITIVE!

The more attention we give to a thought or idea, the stronger it becomes. As we plan our life's activities, we can give either positive or negative attention to each situation. That which receives positive attention will grow in a positive direction. Whatever receives negative attention will become more strongly negative. For example, striving positively to recover from your personal loss will result in progress toward your goal of recovery. On the other hand, feeling negative and hopeless about your recovery will pull you away from that goal. Positive thinking spurs you on. Negative thinking holds you back. Positive attention to your life gives you energy, negative attention takes it away.

Plan for positive outcomes.

Whatever steps you take to restore your health, plan a positive outcome for each activity. Look forward to profiting from your efforts. A positive expectation produces positive results.

Turn your depression into a cleansing force.

It's O.K. to feel depressed and it's important to express that depression. However, in doing so be careful not to dwell on your sadness and pain. Cry long enough to release your emotions, then pick yourself up and move on.

Use your pain as a tool for recovery.

Pain is the beginning of the healing process. It is acceptable as a guest, but not as a long-term visitor. Recognize your pain, accept it, question it, then use the answers to those questions to move along the road to recovery.

RELIEVE YOUR ANGER

Once you have recognized your anger, it is crucial to let the anger out of your system. People usually suppress anger hoping it will disappear and they won't have to deal with it. It's possible to withhold anger for years. But the problem that arises is two-fold: 1) anger turned inward can eat away at your own system causing impatience, arguments, overreaction, ulcers, headaches, and overall increased tension; or 2) angers that are shut away for long periods of time can build on each other to one day erupt like a volcanic explosion often resulting in dangerous or harmful acts toward others. It is easy to see the destructive force behind bottled up anger. It is also easy to understand the importance of releasing those angers as they occur. The advantage here is the great relief you feel after you have let go of angry feelings. Therefore, it is in your best interest to find ways to relieve your anger.

It's O.K. to be angry.

Everyone gets angry when there is a personal loss. Everyone! It is a healthy, human emotion that, when accepted and expressed, enables one to heal. So, let yourself be angry.

It's O.K. to be angry at someone or something.

There will always be an object of your anger — a person or thing. Figure out who or what that object is. It might be the person who died and left you, the person whom you think is responsible for taking the deceased away (like the doctor, or God), a social custom that might have caused your loss (a war that took your son's life), or fate itself.

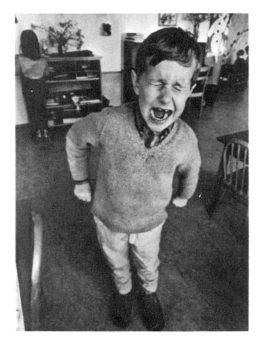

It's O.K. to get angry.

Deal with your anger.

Don't worry about your anger — deal with it. The anger is there. It's not going to go away, and you must accept that fact before you can do anything about it.

Release your anger.

Here are some ideas for discharging your anger. You might feel silly doing some of these, but you will be surprised at the enormous amount of relief you will feel.

1. Hit a pillow.
2. Kick a bed.
3. Cry.
4. Yell and scream. (Your car parked in a deserted area makes a good scream chamber.)
5. Play a competitive sport.
6. Hit a punching bag.
7. Play an instrument as loud as you can.
8. Write your feelings on paper. (If you are angry at the doctor, for example, write a letter to him but don't mail it. Put it away for several months. When you read it later, you will probably find the letter too harshly written.)

Don't let your anger destroy.

It is *not* O.K. to hate yourself or turn your anger into destruction. Remember, the longer you suppress your anger, the more likely it will build into a negative force. Think of how you would feel if you had done something destructive out of anger. You probably would regret it later. Release your anger in a positive fashion. That is the only way you can grow toward a free existence.

TAKE CARE OF YOUR BODY

The process of healing occurs when the many aspects of your personal being are pulled together and interwoven into a fabric of good health. We have talked about your mind and emotions. Now we must attend somewhat to your physical well-being. Caring for your bodily needs has everything to do with your ability to heal. You must have physical strength to achieve inner strength so proper nutrition is the first order of the day. All living things need a certain amount of food to live well. This can be readily observed in a plant that receives no water. Slowly, the weakened leaves curl under until they finally droop to the ground. The same thing can happen to people who fail to eat a proper diet, only in a more subtle way. However, the weakening effects of a poor diet in a human being are not as easy to see as they are in the shrinking plant. Thus, it is hard to know when the body needs better food.

Another obstacle to good health is an addictive habit or activity. Addictions not only disturb your mind, they break down your body's energy and vitality. Be kind to your body as well as your mind. Be aware of the effects of a poor diet and an addictive habit by giving some thought to the following:

Maintain a regular diet.

If you eat regularly, keep on doing so. If you do not have regular eating habits, try to arrange three balanced meals per day. DO NOT CRASH DIET during your period of bereavement. Good nutrition speeds the healing process.

Eat nutritious foods.

Each day should supply you with nutrition from each of the four major food groups: 1) meat, poultry, and fish, 2) dairy products, 3) fruits and vegetables, and 4) breads and cereals. Increase your intake of protein (fish, meat, eggs, etc.), calcium (dairy products), and potassium (potatoes, parsley, bananas). Take a B-vitamin and C-vitamin supplement and a multi-vitamin mineral supplement to build your body's ability to fight stress. Be sure to check with your doctor before using these supplements.

Limit junk foods.

Junk foods can give you a sudden spurt of energy but not a lasting energy. They temporarily fill your stomach (which helps fill the emotional void you're feeling) but they are really only calories with little nutrition. It might be difficult to completely give up eating junk foods if they are already a large part of your diet, but try to decrease the amount and replace them with nutritious foods.

Beware of addictive habits.

Be careful about anything that can be addictive. A personal loss leaves you vulnerable to false securities which might tempt you to increase your use of cigarettes, alcohol, or drugs. It's up to you to be on the lookout for activities that will give you a quick "high." These substances allow you only a temporary escape or relief from your suffering. Then, when the high goes away, the pain returns. Stay with your pain and work through it — don't run away from it.

Watch your alcoholic intake.

You may consider yourself just a social drinker, but the escape you get from being high might feel good enough to repeat — it can become habit-forming. Alcohol might numb the pain momentarily, but it *is* a depressant that can eventually throw you into a deeper depression.

Be careful about drugs.

Social drugs (marijuana, cocaine, speed, etc.) can bring your healing process to a screeching halt. Like alcohol, a series of temporary highs will lead to a depression that can be deeper than your earlier despair. Once again, you must feel and deal with your pain if you are to recover. Drugs are a way of avoiding that pain.

Follow your doctor's advice on medication.

Medication is to be avoided unless your doctor prescribes it. Sedatives or tranquilizers are in order *only* if your doctor has approved them as part of your overall recovery program.

RECORD YOUR THOUGHTS AS YOU RECOVER

As you take your first step toward recovery, keep a journal or diary to record your thoughts while you are healing. This activity can help you to learn and understand more about yourself. As you read what you have written, it will be easier to place your feelings in proper perspective. Those overwhelming feelings of sadness and loss may diminish as you reread and understand your thoughts about them. These few points will help get you started:

Put your thoughts and feelings on paper.

Writing down your thoughts and feelings will make them more concrete, therefore easier to understand. If you have trouble putting your feelings into words, try showing how you feel by drawing pictures. This can be as effective as writing.

Write only when you feel like it.

Do not force yourself to write. Write only when it feels appropriate so your thoughts flow readily.

Look for signs of recovery.

As your healing progresses, you will find that:

1. You feel more alive,
2. Your thinking is sharper,
3. Your concentration is improved,
4. Your judgment is more reliable, and
5. Your view of the world is open, positive, and involves others.

Perfection of means and confusion of goals seems in my opinion to characterize our age.
— *Albert Einstein*

- Make Changes
- Be Forgiving
- Help Others
- Let the Past Brighten Your Future
- Discover Your Creative Self

MAKE CHANGES

As you outline your program for a healthy recovery, be sure to set goals for yourself so you can see your growth throughout the healing process. Without goals, your efforts can be a grind because you have no measure of achievement. With goals, even the most routine activity will show its purpose. Plan goals within your reach so you have a continuing sense of achievement. The **Steps for Survival** and **Habits for Healing** in this guide book will help you set some of your goals. In addition, the goals for change that are mentioned here can work for you as well:

Prepare to make adjustments.

If you are to grow and heal, you will have to make changes in your thinking and manner of living. Prepare to make changes in your habits, your relationships with others, and your general life style. Reassessing your values might become a continuing need throughout your life in order to keep growing. Once you stop changing and your existence becomes stale, you are a prime target for depression. It will take courage, but if you can accept and adjust to change, you will find life to be an exciting adventure.

Be open to new experience.

Try to keep an open mind when you are introduced to new people, places, ideas and experiences. Just because something is unfamiliar to you or different from what you already know doesn't mean it is undesirable. Some things you will like, some things you won't like. Try out something new for the sake of those things you *will* like.

Be trusting.

Be curious. Be willing to learn. Then trust the future to bring unknown experiences that will make your life better. Instead of being afraid of unfamiliar situations, try taking some risks. And, most important of all, trust your ability to adapt to new ideas and events.

Try something new.

Renew the "trappings" of your life style.

To aid in your adjustment to a new life, try making simple changes in your life like redecorating, buying new clothes, or allowing yourself that special luxury you've always wanted. These kinds of changes can give you a fresh start.

Accentuate your positives.

Use your own good qualities to make a more satisfying life. Try to be more:

- helpful
- concerned
- trusting
- tolerant
- giving
- loving

Above all, be yourself!

BE FORGIVING

Showing forgiveness is not always easy to do. There might be anger, resentment, or bitterness standing in the way of your ability to forgive. Take time to think through your anger, express your feelings about it, and try to view it in a positive light with these thoughts:

Forgive yourself.

As soon as you can, forgive yourself for any wrongdoings you think you have caused. Remember that no one is perfect nor can anyone ever expect to be perfect. Go easy on yourself and maintain your self-esteem.

Forgive the other person.

As mentioned earlier, you might be holding resentment for the doctor who cared for the deceased, angry at the

. . . countless ways to help others.

deceased for dying, or bitter toward an outside force for allowing this death to occur. No matter who it is or how you feel, it is important to forgive that person. Keeping angry, resentful feelings inside can only cause added turmoil.

Ensure your forgiveness through kindness.

To forgive is more than to pardon: it is to return good for wrong. Even though you feel you have been wronged, an act of kindness on your part will show the other person you are truly forgiving. This will tell him/her you no longer hold a grudge. This is the only kind of forgiveness that can lessen your anger.

HELP OTHERS

Pulling yourself out of deep despair is often a difficult task. Although no quick remedy is available, there is an activity that can take your mind off your sorrows and create good feelings within you. Think of someone who needs help, even in some small way. Call that person on the phone to offer your time, companionship, labor or other assistance. Spending your time as a helpmate will divert your attention from the pain of your loss. That person's appreciation for your help can do wonders for your self-esteem.

Extend a helping hand.

Helping others will occupy your mind, turning you away from self-pity. There are countless ways to help others. Here are just a few:

1. Drive someone to the grocery store.
2. Tune-up a friend's car.
3. Volunteer to take calls at the local drug center, rap line, hot line, etc.
4. Become a "big brother" or "big sister."
5. Visit someone in the hospital.
6. Do housework for an older person.
7. Read to the blind.

8. Talk to the lonely.
9. Listen to the ignored.

Share the joy of giving.

Giving to others is one of life's greatest pleasures. Reaching out to help someone in need is the purest form of giving. It provides a great sense of satisfaction and purpose. Share this joy by investing your personal time and energy in another person's life.

LET THE PAST BRIGHTEN YOUR FUTURE

Everyone's past holds a wide range of experiences that have proven to be either good or bad, profitable or unprofitable, helpful or useless. Out of these experiences, it is important to draw from those positive ideas and activities to improve the quality of future living. Events of the past can serve us well in preparing for the future.

Learn from the past.

There are many lessons we can learn from both the positive and negative events of our past. We can remember what worked and what didn't work using that knowledge to create a more efficient, more effective means of living in the future.

Learn your strengths and weaknesses from the past.

Allow the past to teach you about yourself. Face your good and bad features honestly. Put your feelings aside so you can learn how to focus your energies in a positive direction.

Reflect on the past, don't dwell on it.

Memories of the past can drift into your mind unexpectedly. These memories will remind you of where you have been. Reflect on them, don't dwell on them. Let these memories show you how far you have come.

Death awareness enables maximum living.

DISCOVER YOUR CREATIVE SELF

As you learn and understand more about dealing with death, you will better acquaint yourself with the meaning of life. Death motivates you to re-evaluate how you have been living. It prompts you to take a hard look at your values and priorities and rearrange them to achieve a richer, fuller life. In doing this, you become more aware of the beauty, the purity, and the essence of life. As your thoughts reach into the center of your being, you will discover a creative force within you that you never knew existed.

As you recover, note how you have changed.

Weathering the crisis of your personal loss has made you stronger, wiser, more sensitive, and more independent. You are different than you used to be because you have grown and matured into a more complete human being. Free of the controls of pain and depression, you can finally live the joy and happiness of a meaningful life.

Exercise your creativity.

Now that you have a deeper insight into the substance of life, select an art form that will allow you to express your creativity. Write, sing, dance, paint, sew, build, design. Let your creative energy flow. Use this energy to make your world one of maximum living.

About the Author:

Dr. John Canine did his doctoral dissertation on death, dying, and bereavement at Wayne State University in Detroit, Michigan. He is currently director of Maximum Living Counseling Center in Birmingham, Michigan.

PHOTOS REPRINTED FROM "THE FAMILY OF WOMEN"

Cover Photo .... U.S.A., Bill Binzen
Page 6 .... Top Photo — ENGLAND, Julian Calder/Woodfin Camp (pg. 180)
Page 6 .... Bottom Photo — DENMARK, Gregers Nielsen (pg. 76)
Page 19 .... WEST GERMANY, Bernard Pierre Wolff (pg. 161)
Page 35 .... Top Photo — U.S.A., Eugene Richards/Magnum (pg. 146)
Page 35 .... Bottom Photo — U.S.A., Suzanne Szasz (pg. 147)
Page 53 .... Top Photo — U.S.A., John Avery (pg. 138)
Page 53 .... Middle Photo — U.S.A., Jim Mendelhall (pg. 138)

PHOTOS REPRINTED FROM "THE FAMILY OF CHILDREN"

Page 23 .... Top Photo — ANGOLA, J. P. Laffont/SYGMA (pg. 144)
Page 23 .... Bottom Photo — ANGOLA, J. P. Laffont/SYGMA (pg. 144)
Page 28 .... U.S.A., Brian Lanker (pg. 155)
Page 30 .... Top Photo — U.S.A., Zeva Oelbaum (pg. 155)
Page 30 Bottom Photo — CYPRUS, Donald McCullin/MAGNUM (pg. 155)
Page 38 .... U.S.A., Suzanne Szasz (pg. 71)
Page 43 Top Photo — FRANCE, Phelps/Rapho-Photo Researchers (pg. 44)
Page 46 .... SWEDEN, Nils-Johan Norenlind/TIO (pg. 114)
Page 53 .... Bottom Photo — U.S.A., Joe Rainaldi (pg. 115)
Page 55 .... BANGLADESH, J. P. Laffont/SYGMA (pg. 79)
Page 58 .... U.S.A., Ron Engh (pg. 111)

PHOTO REPRINTED FROM "TO LIVE UNTIL WE SAY GOODBYE"
(Elizabeth Kubler-Ross)

Page 13 .... Jack, St. Rose Home-Watering Flowers (pg. 123)

NOTES